Albert Labbett's CREDITON COLLECTION II

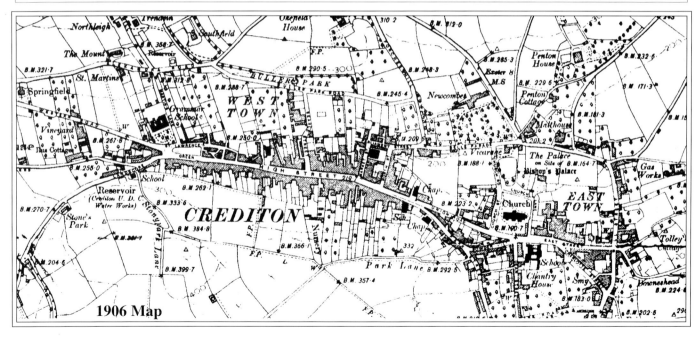

1906 Map

Other Books in this Series
Albert Labbett's Crediton Collection
An Alphington Album, *P. Aplin & J. Gaskell*
The Dawlish Collection, *Bernard Chapman*
The Totnes Collection, *Bill Bennett*
Pictures of Paignton, *Peter Tully*
Pictures of Paignton Part II, *Peter Tully*
Ian Jubb's Exeter Collection
Dartmoor in Colour, *Chips Barber*
Exeter in Colour, *Chips Barber*
Torbay in Colour, *Chips Barber*
Plymouth in Colour, *Chips Barber*

For further details of these or any of our extensive Devon titles, please contact us at 2 Church Hill, Pinhoe, Exeter, EX4 9ER, Tel: (0392) 68556.

ISBN: 0 946651 69 8

Other Obelisk Publications
The Lost City of Exeter, *Chips Barber*
Diary of a Dartmoor Walker, *Chips Barber*
Diary of a Devonshire Walker, *Chips Barber*
Adventure Through Red Devon, *R. B. Cattell*
Under Sail Thr S Devon & Dartmoor, *R. B. Cattell*
The Great Walks of Dartmoor, *Terry Bound*
The A to Z of Dartmoor Tors, *Terry Bound*
The Great Little Dartmoor Book, *Chips Barber*
The Great Little Exeter Book, *Chips Barber*
Made in Devon, *Chips Barber & David FitzGerald*
Tales of the Unexplained in Devon, *Judy Chard*
Haunted Happenings in Devon, *Judy Chard*
Dark & Dastardly Dartmoor, *Sally & Chips Barber*
Weird & Wonderful Dartmoor, *Sally & Chips Barber*
Ghastly & Ghostly Devon, *Sally & Chips Barber*
The Ghosts of Exeter, *Sally & Chips Barber*
Ten Family Walks on Dartmoor, *Sally & Chips Barber*
Ten Family Walks in East Devon, *Sally & Chips Barber* (Harback)
More... Cobblestones Cottages & Castles, *David Young*

First Published in 1993 by Obelisk Publications
2 Church Hill, Pinhoe, Exeter, Devon
Designed by Chips and Sally Barber
Typeset by Sally Barber
Printed in Great Britain by
Sprint Print Co Ltd, Okehampton Place, Exeter

© **Albert Labbett 1993**
All Rights Reserved

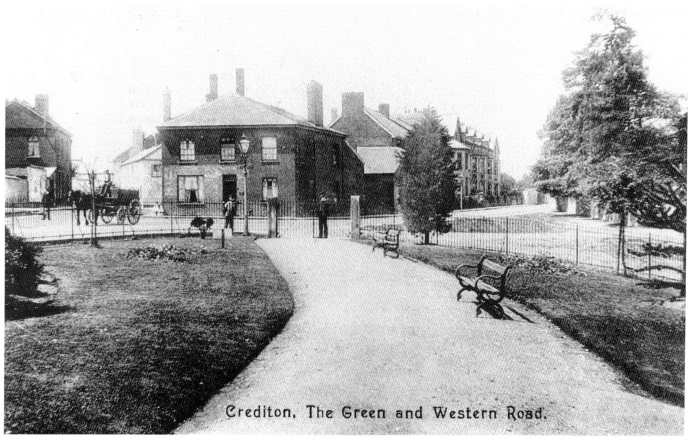

Crediton, The Green and Western Road.

We start our nostalgic look at Crediton with a sad story. This picture shows The Green and Western Road. It was here at the times of the Napoleonic Wars that Mary Ann Rosslyn was seduced by a young French officer who was placed in the town as a prisoner of war. At the end of the hostilities, when he was free to return to his own country, he persuaded her to elope to London with him but he abandoned her. She managed to get home to Crediton with the help of a kindly magistrate only to find her father on his death bed with her mother soon to follow. It was all too much for her so she went down to the River Creedy and drowned herself.

Before 1890 The Green was an open space where fairs, church gatherings and other events took place. In May of 1847, when the poor of the town were starving, a man named Martin snatched a pitchfork and plunged it into a stock of bread withdrawing a 4lb loaf. This incident started a riot, the mob shouting "we are starving" assembled on The Green and broke into every food shop encountered. Two hundred special constables were needed before the situation was brought under control late in the evening. Three years later a party of workers engaged on the North Devon Railway project, unable to work because of the hard frost, roamed the streets of Crediton shouting "Give us Bread". Not only were the shops looted, but the shopkeepers were pelted with stones!

Not far from The Green is a scene showing a street market held in 1880. The carts brought in litters of pigs to be sold. To stop them escaping nets were placed over the top. The pub on the extreme right was The Dock Inn which closed after 1950 when Mr A. Bicknell was the landlord.

This scene of great activity shows soldiers emerging from North Street whilst participating in a cross-country run. This was part of their training to make them ready to face action in France. Some of the local children have joined in the race, the soldiers being not much older.

Flags and decorations in November 1900 were displayed all over the town to welcome home General Buller, Corporal Berry and Private Lethbridge from the Boer War. Lethbridge was met at the railway station and then taken in procession to the Public Rooms, there being presented with a gold watch subscribed for by the working men of the town. Corporal Berry had taken his discharge in South Africa and had received his watch there.

The Royal Order of Crediton Buffaloes had their headquarters at the "The Duke of York". Here the parade is passing Ernest Jackson's sweet factory, now Redvers House, in Union Road. The town band with Art Setter (Bandmaster) in Trilby hat and Fred Harvey beside him led the parade to the church for their service with the Vicar of Crediton, then the Rev Richards. Two people known in the parade are Jack Motley and Arch Purse. The chap by the ladies' toilet sign is Walt Frost. The photo was taken after the Second World War being dated by the missing railings outside the factory and Wesleyan Church, these having been taken to make war munitions.

This Church outing scene at Union Road in 1913 shows mostly women with a few small boys sitting on the floor of the carriages. They would probably have visited Fingle Bridge. In later years the most common annual outing of church and chapel would be a train journey to Exmouth. On such occasions Crediton was almost deserted.

This very old photo of 1865 is dated by the period dress. It shows the name of C. Herring on the board over the door. It was a puzzle to locate where this building stood. However, a search through the census records between 1841 and 1881 reveals that it is the grocer's shop of Govier near The Green. For many years the building housed a bakery where there was once a fire. Fireman Wollacott collapsed and died on the fire station floor beside the ladder which he had been sent to fetch.

Sir Redvers Buller had seen service in Canada, China and Ashanti before he won The Victoria Cross in Zululand. This picture shows his coffin being placed on the gun carriage at his funeral in 1908. He was buried in the North East corner of Crediton Churchyard.

The day the wall came down! This former tree-lined road is shown here many years ago with workmen gazing towards the photographer. Behind them is now the war memorial, a familiar landmark in Crediton which pays homage to all those men who gave their lives for King and Country. Many of the names recorded were those of men who served in the Devonshire Regiment. Almost six thousand men in the regiment gave their lives in the First World War. Public conveniences now lie behind the point where the wall was at its tallest in this picture.

There were two ponds where the Bowling Green now stands, filled by a stream which ran in an open drain from The Green at the top of the town. Added to it was a considerable volume of manure from the town! The stench from it was such that Benjamin Cleave of Newcombes House sought a legal settlement, but was unsuccessful.

The Minutes of the old Court Leet (1811) alluded to this aspect of Civic Hygiene: "Ordered that Mary Slee and Grace Howard do cease throwing their nuisances in or near a public highway on Forfeit of 10 shillings." This photo, with just one lady amongst many men, possibly shows the opening ceremony.

"Winswood", Crediton

The Prayer Book Rebellion started when English had to be read in all churches on Whit Sunday in 1549. The Rebellion began at Sampford Courtenay, and spread quickly. Sir Peter and Sir Gawan Carew were ordered to quell it with troops from the Garrison at Exeter. They marched to Crediton where the rebels manned the barns here at Winswood. Sir Peter sent his soldiers to storm the barns where they were met with showers of arrows. It was only when the barns were set alight that the rebels took to their heels. As a punishment to the town, the clappers of the church bells were removed and were not replaced for another twenty years!

Lawyer Stone built Newcombes, on the edge of town, in 1741. It has had various owners. The Cleaves added the columns of granite, the stone having been brought from the Blackingstone Quarries near Daccombe on the Exeter to Moretonhampstead road. During the Second World War the London-based film company, Gaumont British, occupied the grounds and built a row of chalets for their staff. The house was demolished and now this is the location of a doctor's surgery and car park.

(Opposite) The old cob cottages of Fountain Court were originally thatched, and were where weavers toiled with their looms from sunrise to sunset. In winter they used disused tan bark for fuel which, when burnt, smelt awful. With no back door or windows for ventilation to the cottages, it must have been an unpleasant working environment.

(Right) By order of the Privy Council in 1574, the Master of the Posts arranged a change of horses at all the convenient places for the speeding up of mail. In stark contrast to today's postal code for sorting out the mail, the directions for those early deliverers would have run something like this: Philip Buckingham – At ye Greene; Artstarus Drake – Up ye towne; John Border – In Bowden Hill; Valurous Thorne – At ye towne end; William Wonymyll – In ye park; John Please – In ye West towne. In later years when the London mail came to Crediton, the area was divided into eight rides for the postboys. An extra penny was charged for these deliveries, hence the Penny Black Stamp came into being. This picture shows the local team of postmen, some of them mere boys!

(Above) The streets are crowded and people are hanging out of the windows to witness the Coronation Day celebrations of 1911. It was a time in Crediton where everyone knew everybody else and an occasion like this was regarded as a social occasion of the highest order. It was also a time when the children had a good wash behind the ears and put on their Sunday best!

(Opposite) The large building on the left, which is now a furniture shop, was originally 'The Public Assembly Rooms'. The funds to build it were raised by general subscription and Gould of Barnstaple was its architect and builder. The foundation stone was laid by Mr J.W. Buller's eldest son. To collect money for the furniture and fittings, a fancy fair was promoted, one of the best ever seen in Kirton. Creedy Park was the setting and Mrs Buller and her three daughters supervised its production. In later years it became a cinema with old Dick Sprague the Town Crier shouting outside about the films "From all over the world – and other places too". I don't know where he thought that was!

This photo shows Mr Rippin with daughter Blanche at their shop at 72 High Street, Crediton. Here they sold produce from their farm at Denbury. Their farm was a haven for young boys who collected birds' eggs. The marsh between the farm and the river was the nesting place for duck, plover, snipe and moorhen.

The premises of J.W. Murch, a tailor, could have been at or near the dwelling of Mr Cobley where the greatest fire of Crediton started on August 14th 1743, a Sunday morning. Fourteen bodies were recovered whilst several others were missing. 460 houses were left in ruins, leaving over 2,000 homeless. They lost everything including their looms. Mr Cobley left the town never to return. One of these men was so curious to see the blowing up of a house to stop the fire spreading that he went too close and was killed by the explosion. A collection throughout the country was made for the relief of Crediton. Moore's Garage is shown next door with its four petrol pumps huddled together in the old style that filling stations once exhibited.

(Left) To provide an area for the market, the Town Improvement Act of 1839 was passed by the Lord of the Manor, Mr Buller (a Member of Parliament) to demolish part of Parliament Street, then known as 'the Back Lane', and to widen it as far as Belle Parade. An old custom was revived which stated that no corn in bulk, poultry, or dairy produce, fish or meat could be sold in the town, on Saturdays, elsewhere than in the market. As late as 1911, Cox, a long established butcher, was fined 20 shillings for contravening this manorial right.

(Opposite) This is Fred Salter in the doorway of his fish and chip shop at 107 High Street which he ran with his wife. Before them Bill Deem ran the business. The original owner was Sam Gearing who also toured the town with his mobile hand cart selling fish and chips.

This fine photograph shows a small convoy of wagons about to leave Crediton. On board are members of the First Crediton Volunteer Company (Devonshire Regiment) their destination being Haldon for their annual camp. The proceedings have obviously created a great deal of local interest as a small crowd has assembled to give them a good send off.

The star of the Crediton Carnival of 1911 was "The Bear", featured in this photograph. The assembled crowd is portrayed outside Nos 5 and 6 The High Street. Some of the advertisements in the windows of Holman Ham, the family chemists, and Berry, the Hairdresser and tobacconists, make interesting reading!

This is John Moore outside the garage, opposite Oxford Terrace, in Mill Street which he ran with his brother George. John served with the Seventh Cyclists Battalion in France, and repaired the cycles. After the war the brothers started their repair works, starting with cycles, which were hired out for 6d a day. They graduated to motor cycles (Triumph) and then on to cars. On leaving Mill Street the business moved to High Street, next to 'The White Swan' and later on to Bank House which they converted into the present garage which is still run by the Moore family.

The White Hart, shown here in all its glory, can claim one unusual distinction. At a meeting here over two centuries ago, local chemist Richard Lathy, was ordered to be prosecuted for failing to pay the necessary toll to pass along the section of road between this hotel and Newton St Cyres. He was let through on trust but later refused to pay. This little drama was played out on 29th October 1764.

What has four solid wheels, a driver called Marles and can travel up to the great speed of 12 mph? The answer is this splendid conveyance which belonged to John Cleave and Son Ltd of Crediton. In 1879 John Cleave established a business at East Street (where the Potters Snooker club is now located) and manufactured Cholene (Chocolate and Honey) and Butterscotch. The lorry is shown here in nearby Church Lane.

Four Mills in Crediton is aptly named for at one time it had four mills – two were grist and two were flour. Alas mills are always prone to catch fire and these did in spectacular fashion. By the time the Insurance Brigade had arrived from Exeter the building had been reduced to a glowing shell. The site is now a garage, situated close to the level crossing over the railway.

Here we see the fire brigade showing off their new engine to the townspeople in the late 1930s outside the White Swan Hotel. The building with a wrought iron balcony was an iron monger's shop, but later Moore's garage transferred to this site from their Mill Street premises.

This was Crediton's solid tyre first motor fire engine. Left to right at the back are Wilf Parker (Driver), W. Discombe (the Landlord of the Oatsheaf Hotel), Joe Hill (a Mason). Front: Left to right, Parry Jones (a Bank Manager who lived at the Chantry), Dean Street (the Chief Officer), George Burrows second officer (who kept the White Hart Hotel). The original alarm for the firemen was blown by a Bugler sounding the call. This was replaced by a maroon set off at the War Memorial by the Engineer of the Brigade, Mr Cherry. Old Kyrtonians would remember the old ditty.

'Fire, fire,' Mr Dyer
'Where to,' said Mr Drew
'Up the town,' said Mr Down
'It's out to Sturridge'
said Mr Burridge.

Mill St was so named after the Four Mills (previously mentioned) near the railway level crossing. The Star Inn, to the right of the horse and cart, was well placed for travellers and pack horse convoys coming from Exeter via Commonmarsh Lane on the main route to Barnstaple, via Sandford, Morchard and South Molton. In 1701 it was referred to as "Ye Star" in the occupancy of Ye Widow Tucker. The last landlord was Mr Hammett when the Star Inn finally closed in 1926.

This was the main road from Exeter through the town before Charlotte Street and Union Street were made. Looking down Park Road from Dean Street entrance towards Exeter Road, parts of the left hand wall still remain but the right hand side has completely changed. From Winswood House to the cottage, where Arthur Richardson lived, by Hunivers Lane was a long stretch of trees about 25 yards wide, then opening out to a meadow, now the Winswood Estate. Arthur Richardson was well known throughout the country as a maker of violins and violas. Many could often be seen hanging from his clothes line to dry after coats of varnish had been applied to them!

The name Blagdon appears in several road names in Crediton. Peter Blagdon, the Squire of Puddington, came to live here in 1816 and the locality adopted his name. Edward, his only son, when a cadet of 17 on a voyage to India, was forced to fight a duel with an aggressive ship's Officer. Coming safely out of that scrape, he was posted to Barisal in Bengal, but he alas was dead and buried within twelve months. The Blagdon property thereupon went to an only daughter, the wife of William Hornsey Gamlen of Tiverton, whose grandson sold Blagdon House in 1919. The thatched cottage on the left has gone. It was demolished in an unusual way (see Crediton Collection).

Floods occurred regularly at Fordton before the flood relief scheme came into operation. Mr Ridge of 'Ridge and Webber' the local milkmen in East Street is seen delivering milk to Fordton shop on 5 December 1929. Brick piers were erected and planks of wood placed on top to form a cat walk for people to walk along Fordton Plain. The girl in the gateway was Joyce Whittaker, the daughter of the golf professional of the old Uton Golf Course. Her mother was the head teacher of Hookway School. The worst floods occurred in the 1960s, when the water from the river covered the whole area to the railway. Flood water even came down the rail track and washed away a bridge at the far end of the present golf course.

The first Carnival Queen after the 1939/45 War was Fred Salter's wife. Sid Ford, the taxi driver, lived at Crownhill Terrace. The Queen's attendants were Miss Martin with hands on face, and Miss Vicary partly obscured. In the early days of the Carnival, boys carried hand-held paraffin torches to escort the Carnival floats through the town, quite different from today with generators lighting the tableaux with very bright lamps.

Abraham Cann of Colebrooke was the Devon champion wrestler. He was 5'8" tall, weighed 12 stone and was very powerful. At Widecombe in the Moor, he met Thorn, also a man of immense strength who, as a Lifeguardsman at Waterloo, cut down ten of the enemy with his own sword. However, in this encounter Cann threw him inside three minutes. Cann's constant companion and wrestling partner was James Stone of Kirton, who was with him in London at Cann's greatest triumph – The Championship of England in 1827. For training he could keep up with the riders in the hunting field, running and jumping across country. He tossed around 56lb weights just for the exercise of it. He married Mary Gorwyn of Coleford at Crediton Church, then they had three children who were baptised in Clannaborough Church between Copplestone and Bow.

Old Crediton was enclosed in a valley of cob walls from Deep Lane, along People's Park, Alexandra Road to Chapel Down Road. This scene, taken from the top of Stony Park Lane in the late 1930s, shows the old cob wall along the dung track from Landscore School to Jackson's Sweet Factory.

This north-westward looking view of the town shows how it has nestled in a natural bowl in the hills. The foreground has changed greatly since this picture was taken and Crediton has spread in several directions. In the foreground is part of the Lord's Meadow Industrial estate which now sprawls away to the right of the picture.

These deer at Shobrooke Park were a lovely sight to see. They were kept in by a tall wire fence which still stands around most of the park. During the last war the deer escaped into the countryside through an open gate. Rabbits were so numerous in the park and surrounding farms that when a corn field was harvested over a hundred rabbits would be caught. Every person, including boys, would be given one and the rest were sent to the Royal Devon and Exeter Hospital! On one occasion, Poacher Billy Shy hovered on the outskirts of a shooting party whilst the birds were dropping. He was kept under observation by the local police and seen to dive into a patch of tall grass, stuff something under his jacket and run off. When caught by the Constable only a bundle of hay was found – the old rascal had the last laugh!

Crediton "Downes". Seat of Sir R. H. Buller.

About 1692 William Gould planned a large house on part of Ware's Down and called it Downes. His eldest son Moses moved in there in 1702. Elizabeth Gould married James Buller of Morval, M.P. for Cornwall, who later became Master of Downes. Her sister, Frances Gould, became the wife of John Tuckfield, M.P. for Exeter. Not only were these gentlemen in opposite political camps, but they forbade their wives, devoted to each other as sisters, ever to speak to one another. Francis Buller, whilst still at school, married Susannah Yarde, he was but sixteen, she was twenty-one and her own mistress. Before Buller of Downes bought the Lordship of Crediton he was already Lord of the Manors of Exwick and St Thomas, Exeter, in which church some of the family are buried.

These days there is a daily mass exodus from Crediton of the army of commuters who work in Exeter. En route they pass through Newton St Cyres, a village which boasts many attractive cottages. These two photographs hark back to the days when the village had four pubs – The New Inn, The Old Inn, The North Devon and The Crown and Sceptre. Only the latter survives. Perhaps it is just as well, for one villager called Will Clattery, in those long gone days, celebrated the annual fete day by getting hopelessly drunk whilst touring the four

pubs. Police Sergeant Lamacraft together with the appropriately named PC Belch were on duty and decided to arrest and remove him to Crediton. Alas this was long before the days of police cars so old Will was initially placed in a wheel-barrow before being transferred onto an open cart. In a state of deep slumber he was secured to the cart by a pig net and shipped to Crediton to sober up in a police cell.

This car belonging to Mr Sanders of Winkleigh was registered in Durham. It travelled by train to Exeter but on the road journey from the station to Winkleigh, the engine boiled over at Copplestone.

At the turn of the century Cheriton Fitzpaine had about the same population as it does today even though there were not as many houses in the village. This was simply because families were far larger. The village was more self-sufficient with a range of shops. Here the village children are nicely lined up for the photographer to capture them for posterity!

Sandford is just two miles from Crediton's station and has many links with its bigger neighbour. This pair of pictures gives an impression of what the village was like in the past. Sandford's market days were few and far between so the farmers of this area depended on Crediton's weekly markets for their trade. Sandford's oldest Fair and market coincided with St Swithin, after whom its church is dedicated. This was traditionally held on the first Monday after 26 July. The Spring Market, also held in the Square, was always on the third Monday in March. Headwear was obviously in fashion for the menfolk in those days!

This was taken during the Second World War with a group of Royal Signal Regiment Soldiers shown to the right of the picture. The Palace Cinema opened in the late 1920s only to be replaced by a snooker club in more recent times. The large building of L.J. Gibbings, the Baker, to the left, sold sweets. The Earl of Portsmouth on his way home from Exeter would stop at Haywards School, go across the road to this Sweet shop and buy a large bottle of sweets. Then he would scatter them along the pavement and laughed to see the boys scrambling for them. When working at Morchard Bishop where the Earl lived, I saw him hit 44 clay pigeons without missing one – brilliant shooting for a man of over 80!